# Curtained Windows

## Lighted Rooms

Prince George Public Library
887 Dominion Street
Prince George, B.C. V2L 5L1
563 - 9251

# Curtained Windows

## Lighted Rooms

*Bal Sethi*

Caitlin Press Inc.
Prince George, B.C.

Copyright ©2001 Bal Sethi

All rights reserved. No part of this publication may be reproduced, stored in a retrieval system of transmmitted in any form, by any means without prior permission of the publisher, except by a reviewer who may quote a passage in a review.

Published by

Caitlin Press Inc.
Box 2387, Station B
Prince George, BC V2N 2S6

Cover and book design by Warren Clark
Cover image, Maxfield Parrish, *Dusk,* © Parrish Family Trust/ASaP and VAGA (New York)/SODART (Montréal) 2001
Cover photograph by Michael Agee

**National Library of Canada Cataloguing in Publication Data**

Sethi, Bal, 1929-
   Curtained windows, lighted rooms

   Poems.
   ISBN 0-920576-86-9

   I. Title
PS8587.E83C87 2001  C811'.6    C2001-910129-5
PR9199.3.S465C87 2001

Caitlin Press gratefully acknowledges the financial support of the Canada Council for the Arts for our publishing program. Similarly, we acknowledge the support of the Arts Council of British Columbia.

Printed in Canada

THE CANADA COUNCIL FOR THE ARTS SINCE 1957 | LE CONSEIL DES ARTS DU CANADA DEPUIS 1957

BRITISH COLUMBIA ARTS COUNCIL
Supported by the Province of British Columbia

*I would like to dedicate this book
to my children Rajiv, Sanjiv and Neetika,
who turned out to be such fine kids
even in my absence.*

BAL SETHI

# CONTENTS

Acknowledgments  ix
Introduction  xi

SECTION ONE :
*Life Goes On*

    Curtained Windows  3
    Life Goes On  4
    Veiled Moon  5
    The Curtain Drop  6
    Where  7
    Reflections  8
    Reflected Glory  9
    A Park Bench  10
    A Parting Gift  11
    Last Ride  12
    Tongue On Fire  13
    Away From Home  14
    Ascent Of Man  15
    Simple Arithmetic  16
    No U-Turns  17
    Letter Box & A Yogi  18
    Assigning Blame  19
    Who Should I Blame  20
    Reply  21
    Known Pathways  22
    Ecology Of Dreams  23
    Gateway To Sunshine  25
    The Blast  27
    A Befitting Memorial  28

SECTION TWO :
*Wind Rose & Thorn*

    Wind, Rose & Thorn  31
    The Wind Cannot Read  32
    After The Downpour  33
    Why & How  34
    Adaptation  35
    Sunflowers  36
    I Love Thorns, Not Roses  37
    Eyes Can Tell Lies  38
    Wanton Breeze  39
    Flowers  40
    Outlooks  41
    Complacency  42
    Silver Lining  43
    Flirtatious Time  45
    Reminder  46
    Bright Effort  47
    Time Watch  48
    A Broken Pledge  49

SECTION THREE :
*Words Left Unsaid*
    A Rainy Night  53
    Crossings  54
    A Changed Focus  55
    Wayside Stop  56
    An End Without Ending  58
    Home For The Holidays  59
    Soul Mates  61
    Clipped Wings  62
    Time Comes Tiptoeing  63
    The Mirror Doesn't Know  64
    A Smile Is A Smile  65
    Adolescence  66
    I'll Err Again  67
    Will You Not Think Of Me  68
    Expressions  70
    Words Left Unsaid  71
    Un-Relieved Pain  72
    A Tear Drop  73

SECTION FOUR :
*Rama Went Away*
    Re-Incarnation  77
    Some Call Him God  78
    Two for One  79
    He Would Meet Us There  81
    The Budda & The Silence  82
    Commotion  83
    Clay And The Potter  84
    No Fixed Address  85
    Slicing The Air  87
    A Matching Game  88
    Roll Call  89
    Putting Reason To Rest  91
    Balance Sheet  92
    Flower & The Seeker  94
    Rama Went Away  95

# ACKNOWLEDGMENTS

I gratefully acknowledge that some of these poems have appeared in **Green's Magazine, The Quest,** and **The Teak Round-Up.**

I wish I could find appropriate words to adequately thank Dr. Dee Horne, English Dept., University of Northern BC, who consented to critically review the manuscript and write an introduction, in spite of a hectic academic schedule. She made useful suggestions, some of which have been gratefully incorporated.

My sincere thanks are also due to Dr. Marianne Ainley of the UNBC for her encouragement and kind help.

A writer is just a medium. The source of thoughts and inspiration are outside of him. Like a flute, a writer becomes an instrument to let music and melody flow through him or her. I am no different. I owe these poems to that invisible source which not only gives me inspiration but also molds these thoughts and ideas into spontaneous, unpremeditated words and expressions.

# INTRODUCTION

I am delighted and honoured to write this introduction to Bal Sethi's newest collection of poetry. Bal is a talented, thoughtful writer. He writes about the natural world as well as matters of the heart with wisdom and insight. The opening poem, for instance, "Curtained Windows" conveys the mystery of life and reminds us of the importance of a sense of wonder, of wakefulness. Reading Bal's poems is like visiting tidal pools; the more one looks, the more one sees and appreciates the mysteries and wonders that life offers.

In his writing, Bal addresses universal themes of love, and loss in refreshing images and contexts. Elegiac poems like "A Rainy Night," "Wayside Stop," " An End Without Ending," and "Crossings" convey the speaker's nostalgia and recollections of friendships and lovers. "Soul Mates" describes the moment of recognition when like-minded souls meet and realize that they share interests, passions.

In "Home for the Holidays," on the other hand, the narrator discovers that his wife has been unfaithful. What was to have been a relaxing holiday visit home turns into a tragic awakening. Here, and in other poems that treat the subject of infidelity, the poet conveys the complexity of human relationships, alluding to the missed opportunities or the dangers of not appreciating the people we care for and the present moment...In "A Smile is a Smile," for example, the poet looks at the hypocrisy and deception practiced by those who are unfaithful.

    Several poems speak about hypocrisy, complacency, and prejudice. "Simple Arithmetic," for instance, poignantly etches the harsh realities of people living in poverty against the superficiality and impoverished minds of economists and politicians; their grand schemes reveal their ignorance of and lack of understanding for the people and conditions in which they live. Politicians and economists do not understand simple arithmetic; if four hands cannot feed the family, then how can two hands supply enough food? "Balance Sheet" also talks about human accountability and speaks about the weight of the past, "the failings and faults of the forefathers." Here, death is a form of release, a respite from world-weariness. "Adaptation" depicts the pain of assimilation. Using nature as an analogy, the speaker describes the dangers of transplanting vegetation and this becomes a metaphor for the pain of cultural dislocation and displacement. "Last Ride" is a painful and searing indictment of racism and prejudice in which the speaker alludes to the man brutally murdered because of the colour of his skin. Bal's poems provoke thought and do not allow readers to remain complacent.

Ordinary daily events become, in the hands of this talented writer, extraordinary. Poems like "Flowers" and "Wanton Breeze" illustrate how life is transitory. Lives are ephemeral; moments of love and beauty are fleeting, yet precious. Short poems like "Reminder" and "Bright Effort" offer memorable images in compressed lines that impress the message through the medium while "Two for One" and other poems convey the importance of seizing the moment, of appreciating life fully, of remaining awake.

Dr. Dee Horne
English Program
University of Northern British Columbia
Prince George, British Columbia

SECTION ONE

*Life*

*Goes*

*On*

## Curtained Windows

Sun rays
streaking through
the clouds

moonbeams
sifting through
the leaves

fragrance
filtering through
the flowers

simple sights

so much mystery

curtained windows
on
lighted rooms

# Life Goes On

There's no one here
and all over the place
a thin gray veil of fog
and grave after grave
in this old abandoned cemetery
wrapped up in deep silence

the weather beaten headstones
and faded unreadable inscriptions
reflect as much of death
as the grim somber graves.

A lone bird
lands on a headstone
moves its beak over the mossy arch
looks around
then flies away
back to bluer skies
and a livelier world.

# Veiled Moon

The veiled moon
bestirs vile images
of passion, whim and circumstance.

The ideas that slice
fingers off a hand,
and fasten them not
into a firm grasp,
defile the veiled moon
with a sanguine spill
like that of the sun.
—the rising or the setting
does it matter at all?—

It is precious blood
—essence of womanhood—
It spills from the female sanctus
trespassed by misguided minds,
vandalized by mistaken manhood.

Sliced fingers are everywhere,
more keep falling off,
and the sad, veiled moon
listlessly gazes on.

# The Curtain Drop

Let death be like
love at first sight
when eyes meet
hearts quiver
and lightning strikes
fast wiping out
the duality's of different beings.

I would hate to be
sick in bed
or bound to a chair
watching every minute
the agony of a year
a fretting maid
half-willing help
the compassion
the despair
of kith and kin,
of people present
with hearts elsewhere.

# Where

Where?
Where would the kids learn?

At home?
Sweet homes
where bitterness rules
and where parents are
at each other's throats.

At schools?
Nation-building places
where confusion reigns
and where teachers are
unsure of their roles.

In society?
Unwalled school of learning
where those who lead
so often mislead
by coating intent with sugar words.

At churches?
Where preachers talk of simplicity
and sing praises of austerity
and live a life of luxury.

Where?
Where would the kids learn?

# Reflections

From the dyke
grandma and I
loved to watch the full moon
as reflected in the water,
were pleased
when we found, reflected,
our own faces too—
one wrinkled and creased,
the other one
pretty and smooth
like that of the moon.

From the dyke
on a full moon night
I still watch reflections—
of the moon and mine
one wrinkled and creased
over seven decades,
the other one
pretty and smooth
still unchanged.

## Reflected Glory

Sunglasses with UV safeguards
help eyes against the sun
also give them a screen
against the prying eyes
of the passers by
when you can resist
to look at the luscious frames
and curvy bodies, scarcely clad
in tantalizing bikinis
passing coquettishly by your side
on a sunny, sandy beach.

Looking direct at the sun
can hurt the careless eye
but like the sun
imaged in the water
those sunbathed radiant bodies
with sun-catcher droplets
of water, or sun-reflecting grains
of sand, clinging longingly
to the arms and legs
are the reflected glory
of the sun
not hurting or stinging
like the direct sun
but soothing, invigorating
for the overzealous, exploring eyes.

## A Park Bench

Sitting on a park bench
she was wondering
how time had flown
as she was watching
her grandson
on the public swings
rather than her son
which she had thought
she had done only
a short while back.

# A Parting Gift

It was the same familiar sight
the backdrop scene of
the distant mountains; dark, thick
growth of trees below
and a few birds in the blue sky
flying in flocks or in pairs

in his large window
the vast landscape outside
with all its colours, sun and shade
and breath-taking loveliness
looked as if framed

he had looked at it
when first moved into the house
and had seen it since
and relished it, for weeks and months
day after day

with eyes riveted on the window
he saw it again today
and let it seep
deep inside him—

for the last time
a faint smile flickered
in his drooping eyes—

the eyelids dropped
and never opened again.

## Last Ride

Chained to the truck
he was dragged—
bruised, bleeding
on a dusty stretch of road
to a cruel, inhuman death,
and dumped in a wayside bush.

He never knew them
did them no wrong
owed them no money
bore them no grudge—
was a simple, humble man
kind, gentle to all.

They did this to him
for an act of Nature
over which he had
no control
for which he had
no choice
for being
of a different colour.

# Tongue On Fire

The sheep bleat and whine
from the barn—

the candle lit in the parlor
is burning, repaying
for its past

its the fat gathered
from their kind
that gives it a form.

it all comes back

its tongue on fire
declares loud & clear
that slaughtered life
comes back
to settle
the unsettled score.

## Away From Home

It's not so much the distance
or the absence that kills,
as it's the uncertainty that fills
the days with wakeful agony
and the nights with sleepless pain,
whether the abducted child is still alive
and whether they shall ever arrive.

Death is the hardest blow to take,
it does, however, make you resign to fate,
and to get on with the rest of life
as best as you possibly can.
But uncertainty sustains a measured hold
that chokes, yet lets you breathe,
it may often ease, but shall never cease.

# Ascent of Man

Shattered glass, twisted metal
heaps of wood, concrete, bricks
lay in indistinguishable mounds
of debris
all over the place
what once was a populated city.

Pipes broken, water contaminated
power grids wiped out
buildings flattened—
no body lived there anymore
no body could.

A flock of birds flew  high
over the city
eyed the devastation
and flew on, wondering
if evolution ever made sense?

## Simple Arithmetic

The young kids in school uniforms
satchels slinging from shoulders
smiling, chatting, frisking to school
look so good and blessed

The old widow's ten year old
trudges to the yarn factory
for a long ten hour shift

The sound of a mother's yearning
and the child's wish for school
get lost in the rumbles
of their empty stomachs

Good intentioned people
probably mean well
but obviously have
no personal experience
of the grueling demands
and pressures
of poverty, want and hunger

They should understand
if four hardworking hands can't
feed two hungry mouths
all things being equal
how can two hands do that
if the child went to school.

## No U-Turns

Highways with U-turns make it easy
for absent minded drivers
or self-absorbed motorists
to rectify their mistake
turn back to the missed spot

he had no such luck
his kids had removed the sign
blocked the space

he took a long turn
and turned
only to find too much time
had elapsed
and no body even remembered
or cared to know who he was

like a stray bird
winging back to his nest
he thought returning on Father's Day
would make things fall in place
blood, like magnet, would
re-connect the severed parts

not unlike a thief sneaking into heaven
he was wrong.

# Letter Box & A Yogi

Such indifference to
the contents
of the mail
delivered to it
belongs in truth
to a true yogi.

Letters of love
or hate,
of life or death
success or set-back
are all the same,
and are received
by it
with non-chalance.

Reaction of the addressee
is however
a different thing—
not being a letter box
or a yogi.

## Assigning Blame

Bridges connect
land with land
people with people

very often though
becomes a passage
to intolerant feet

heavy hands
narrow minds
insensitive hearts

and disconnect
people from people

reversing
human beings
into beasts.

Should one
blame
the bridges?

## Who Should I Blame?

Good results flow from own efforts
things going wrong is all bad luck
there's strange solace and satisfaction
in dumping blame on someone else.

Creditors have no patience to wait
for long overdue payments
neighbours lack love for pets
when they show intolerance
as my cat goes into their backyard
to do her thing.

Post Office never stops delivering notices
for long forgotten unpaid bills
or of neighbours intent to retaliate.

Between the postman and the mailbox
who should I blame?

# Reply

You have called me
a bore
a whore
& a score
of other names,
and have felt pride
in being tall & high.

But I have listened
& kept quiet,
not because
what you said
was right,
but because
words are meaningless,
like hollow sounds,
that emanate
from empty heads.

# Known Pathways

Familiarity breeds contempt.
But don't you forget,
familiarity is safety
like driving daily to work
the same route
without anxiety or fear,
knowing every bend and curve,
like sex with your partner
of a long, cherished time.

# Ecology Of Dreams

Sweet dreams
    are
welcome visitors
the bad ones
uninvited guests.

A surprise kiss
    from
unattainable lips

and unexpected rise
    to
inaccessible heights

a sudden windfall
    from
an obscure source

a complete recovery
    at
unknown hands

cause a shout of delight
    to greet
the images so sweet
even in one's sleep.

No passport handy
    at
customs check

a snake slithering
    in
one's pants

a ferocious foe
    in
hot pursuit

one's axed body
    at
one's door

effect a scream of fright
    and scare
    to escape
even in a nightmare.

Wish there were
    a gadget
in this age
    of reuse
to sift and recycle
repelling nightmares
into welcome dreams
thus helping
in cleaning
the subconscious environs
by turning
the filmy material
of dark shadows
into radiant forms.

## Gateway To Sunshine

There was something about that face
that caught your wandering eye
and anchored it down.

Like layers & layers of fog
her sadness lay impenetrable.

Her eyes were vacant,
with just a fixed stare—
without a stir, motion or change—
windows covered with heavy drapes.

She was a statue, caught & cast
in a moment of deep despair.

The moving world had stopped
in the stillness of that haunted look.
The kids running, bubbling with laughter
& the moms concerned, chasing after,
the old man pausing, coughing and walking,
the young couple mooing, kissing & talking,
were nonexistent, along with the park.

They caused no stir in the silence
of that one constant, vacant look—
like stuck hands of an unmoving clock.

A chubby little boy, with golden curls,
came scampering by & sat next to her.
"Would you have some?" his hand held
a small bag of hot, buttered corn.

She turned her head, saw, unseeing—
the distant look remained still fixed.

"Please take some," followed his mom's voice,
"he loves to share, if you don't mind."

It helped bare a loving sight—
she had such pretty eyes
liquid pools of iridescent hues—
green, blue, no, greenish blue
like nothing that I thought or knew.

The smile that rose in her moistening eyes
was sunshine bursting from cloudy skies.

It lingered, brightened and shone
long after the boy and mom were gone.

You don't need Houdini's with magic wands;
magic lies even in little hands!

## The Blast

I shut my ears—
I still hear the blast
and see limbs and bodies
in pieces, flying all over.

My leg gone
there was no pain
just a numb feeling—
pain was excruciating later
not then.

A door shuts loudly
a log falls with a thud
a rock loosens from the top
lands raucously on the bottom—
every single sound is an associate
of the noise and thunder
of the blast.

I can shut my ears

my ears cannot shut out
the blast.

## A Befitting Memorial

Those who never returned
were as dear to their folks
as those who, whole or not,
came back to their home.

Memorials in various forms
commemorate their sacrifices
and the service they rendered
when their country called.

Every year the Remembrance Day
reminds those who live today
of the cause and the values
they staked their lives for.

They did what they could do.
Its time we do OUR part.
Let their memorial be
For ever a grateful heart!

SECTION TWO

*Wind
Rose &
Thorn*

# Wind, Rose and Thorn

The wind came
shook the rose stem
scattered its petals
scooped its fragrance
laughed at its plunder
and scampered on.

The thorn on guard
was alert, watching
for human hand
little guessing
unfriendly hands
could come
in any form.

## The Wind Cannot Read

The wind
tore the title and the pages
off the open book,
and blew
swirled them high in the air,
and scattered
dropping them everywhere.

The wind couldn't heed
if it was a tree or a book,
a flower bush or a brook.
Whatever came in the wake
of its speed
was supposed to move,
bend or break.

It's in the nature of the wind
to blow
and uproot;
it's natural for a book
open to the rushing wind
to be torn or blown
regardless of its subject or source.

Signs and warnings
"Don't Pluck Flowers"
"Private Property"
"No Trespassing"
are meaningless indeed
as the wind cannot read.

## After The Downpour

Weather smeared windows
Waiting to be cleaned
Of dust, dirt and stains
Get a helping hand
From showers and rains
For a clearer, brighter view.

The deposit of days and weeks
Of despair, pain and hurt
In the bleary eyes
Gets washed
By a downpour of tears—

The rain-washed skies
So often carry
A touch of colour and glow—

The bliss of a rainbow!

## Why & How

A storm wrecks your boat
but a raft keeps you afloat
till you reach the sheltered shore
after days of hunger, thirst & cold –
while others were lost or drowned

you wonder why and how?

Was it a pre-determined thing
we call the appointed hour?
And yours was still unmarked?
Or was it chance?
Luck?

# Adaptation

Nature plants, grows, nurtures
in its own way, at its own pace.

People for some reason or exigency
transplant vegetation
from its natural, ecological habitat
to an environment and conditions
external to it
so often altering thereby
in the process
the properties inherent in it
often ending up with something
unconforming to the old
uncomfortable to the new
a new version
a new breed
somewhat mixed up, confused.

while trying to adjust and adapt
some whither or mope or die
others try, struggle to survive.

Human migrants are no different—
assimilation takes it toll.

# Sunflowers

You can't win
when kith and kin,
pals and friends,
for selfish ends,
cast you aside,
with hurt pride,
and sneak close
to all those
who hold power
for the hour.

Should people run
after the sun
for borrowed hours,
like sunflowers?

# I Love Thorns, Not Roses

I love thorns, not roses
as thorns pierce the flesh
and prick the sleeping soul
into vigilant wakefulness.

Dewy leaves of the roses fresh
dance with the tipsy breezes
and the drops of dew that fall
sing with the rustling grasses,
and lull the mind and senses
into languourous drowsiness.

Soft petals of the roses red
on the green and tender twigs
glisten with the morning sun,
and the spell of melting hues
dazzles the gullible eyes,
and dupes the credulous mind.

Oh, not for me, these roses sweet
whose colours mislead the eyes;
no, not for me, these roses soft
whose smell aberrates the mind.
These thorns are so dear to me
for they prick me out of languor
and out of credulous belief.

I love thorns, not roses.

## Eyes Can Tell Lies

Reality can belie comprehension.
At times, we can't see the deception
that the senses play on our perception,
like in an ocean scene
where the foam and the waves are seen
not as one but as separate things,
even though one is the water in turmoil,
and the other the turmoil in water—
water is water, in all forms and shapes
and even when the senses err and falter,
the reality doesn't change or alter.

## Wanton Breeze

She frisks over the stream
and the ripples rise
to touch her feet.
She hums among the trees
and the leaves stir
and join her tune.
She dances over the field
and the crops sway
and keep her beat.
She gambols in the sky
and the clouds advance,
encurl her feet.

She is of the air, ethereal,
she's like a dream, unreal!

You cannot catch, enfold her,
you cannot touch or hold her,
you can only feel her breath
c-o-o-ing along your ear
or whistling through your hair.

# Flowers

Flowers—
such pretty things
to see, smell and touch
that remind you of
the sun, the breeze, the showers
of Nature's care & kindness.

Could these flowers
pinned to the lapels
or buttonholes,
nestling close to beating hearts,
instill a flutter of simple joy,
a spirit of silent sacrifice
and the steady smile & daintiness
of their own ephemeral lives,
into the wearers' indifferent hearts,
perhaps the world could then become,
in a measure, however small,
a better place for all.

## Outlooks

The turbulence in the heart
of uproarious waves
works havoc
on the ocean and the land
sinking ships, eating up shores,
dies down only
after venting out
on the outside world
its fury and rage.

The understreams flow
quietly, unseen
and though their waters
are always in constant motion
they silently absorb within
any surge or stirring,
they lacerate
their own insides
don't agitate the shores.

# Complacency

Toxic emissions
pollute the atmosphere
touching human, plant
and marine life everywhere

No single part
of the world is safe
it's difficult to divide
the air

And yet
we are sitting
and partying
on the top of a mountain
feeling safe
not hearing the rumblings
inside the mountain
about to wake up
from sleep.

## Silver Lining

The wind picked up speed
the powerful gusts
whipped and lashed
upturned cars, unhinged sheds
tore off branches, uprooted poles
till suddenly the lights went out
and the whole town was plunged in
    thick darkness.

An hour or so
with passion spent, the wind slowed
    down,
and gradually huffed and puffed to a
    halt.

In a town accustomed to uninterrupted
    light
there was a rare sense of mystery
in such complete, thick darkness
outside her home—

she stepped out
and gazed at the sky—
a breath-taking sight!

the night stood naked
with its luminous body
sparkling with the sheen of a thousand
        stars.

Her eyes moistened
her heart blessed the outage
for baring such an indescribable scene
which the dazzle of florescent lights
would have kept out of her sight
in her hectic urban life.

## Flirtatious Time

Time flirts with the sun,
and as the sun goes down,
it romances the moon
till the sun returns.

Time is no one's friend—
and there is no end
to its sly moves
and capricious trend.

## Reminder

The earth that lies beneath our feet
rises sometimes in a cloud of dust,
hinting perhaps to forgetful minds
that we are made of the same stuff.

# Bright Effort

Obscurity can't dispel
the dark
but a small flame,
a tiny spark,
can glow & grow
& help lessen the night.

## Time Watch

Time watched then
when the word was given
and a handshake took place
that gave shape to coexistence
over the land and space.

Time watches now
when the word is given,
is still a word—
but an empty sound,
an echo after the flight
of the bird.

Time shall watch
if the bird in flight
shall wing it's way back
to its rightful nest,
and re-affirm the trust
and the good intent.

## A Broken Pledge

From the stream bed
Ophelia said
to Desdemona, lying
on her nuptial bed:

"We are dead—
being victims of
the stupidity
in our own head.

We allowed ourselves
to be led
as man's fools,
as love's tools,
whereas Grandma Eve
had pledged
that her daughters
would rule man
& the man's world
till Time's edge."

"Let's hope,"
Desdemona said,
"our sisters now
shall re-pledge
to clean this smudge,
and thus retrieve
Grandma Eve's name
and her epic image!"

SECTION THREE

*Words*

*Left*

*Unsaid*

## A Rainy Night

The night
I walked alone,
against the conspiracy of light and rain,
overstepping puddles
and a thousand patterns of
shifting shades and light—
with wind rising in whifts, and moaning at times,
I felt my presence by my side—
someone sighed and whispered my name.
It sounded like her voice.

But it was another night
when she and I walked hand in hand
and the rain came cascading down
onto our heads.
But shielded by youth and love,
we laughed, talked and pranced
till she squeezed my arm and reached
up to my dripping ear
and called my name.

I shuddered when someone whispered
my name again
on the lonesome night
when no one was in sight.

I wonder if the spirits visit
their favourite sites
on such deserted nights.

## Crossings

This urn contains the remains of my love.
The gray ashes within is all that's left of her.
How terribly sad it is to admit
that she who sang, danced and loved
lies enclosed in this cheerless pot
reduced to ashes,
and to a muteness, impenetrable.

It is hard for me to reconcile
to the thought that ceases to be.
Is that grace which was named bewitchery,
and the loveliness which eclipsed the moon,
the sweet ringing voice that haunted one in
      dreams
and the lovely eyes where sorcery lived,
enclosed in this mirthless pot,
silenced forever?

My eyes wander in the room
and meet those familiar things
which have been a palpable part of hers
and continue to be.
Her wardrobe is neat and fragrant.
The green sari she hung in the corner
and the coat on the right,

are clean and bright
and expectant of the light touch
of her fair caressing fingers.
On these dear garments of hers
and the things she touched and used
there is a freshness strong as life.
I cannot feel the hand of death
has stolen the animation of her presence.

My eyes wander back to the urn
and an acute pain shoots through me
to see it dumb with the grimness of death
mocking my speculations.

# Wayside Stop

Over the rolling hills
into the green valleys
through arid lands and deserts
villages, towns and cities
under rain, hail, snow, sun
our trip had taken us
through all seasons and scenes
on the familiar highway.

The signposts on the way
are still like pages
of a reference book
intertwining me
at every bend
and stretch of the road
with you,
even though the seat
next to mine now
is bereft of you.

Milestone 250 is now
a vital spot
as I always stop
and step down into the ditch
to place a flower
say a prayer
near a wooden cross
on a mound of stones—
your make-shift cenotaph.

I climb into the car
with a mournful heart
look at the far horizon
and lonesome drive—
then drive on
on the familiar highway
reminiscing about you and me
and the days that shall never be.

## An End Without Ending

You were gone
but your perfume
lingered
in the air
caressing the nose
and nestling inside
the nostalgic mind.

My heart thankful
for the moments
you stopped,
though vivid still
is the scene
of angry exit
when you grabbed
your personal things,
packed your bag
and hurried out.

No parting kiss
not a good-bye—

you had intended
a complete break—

but left behind
your perfumed presence
to tantalize.

# Home for the Holidays

His wife had gone to her sister's home
to help with Christmas baking
with some free time on hand
he went out for a walk
on his favourite beach.

He noticed familiar heel-prints
of special shoes made
for someone's customized needs
and not far from the shore
half sunk in by the sand
still unswept by the tide
a heart-shaped brooch
with his wife's name on it
he had especially got designed
in Italy
shortly after the war.

Now he was home on holidays.

He neared the sheltered rock cave
he used to haunt
in younger days
wanted to pause, reflect
stopped short
the talk and laughter showed
she was there
with another man.

Back home he packed up
his bag—
he had sensed, suspected
heard whispers, subdued talk
but refused to believe it all
for love's sake.

She came home, happy, presuming
all was right
till her eyes fell on his bag—
a shade of guilt shadowed her eyes
she blushed,
and heard him say:
"you shall hear from me"
he put the brooch on the table
picked up his bag
and left.

## Soul Mates

Amidst the crowd
were so many faces
but yours was
so simple, singular
never seen before
never known before.

Your eyes caught mine
for a fleeting second
and you were gone;
something stirred
inside me
and I knew not what,
-a kind of knowing
-a recognition
as if our souls had met
in some other clime
in some other time
you seemed like a lost friend.

Some people we know,
have known for years,
are strangers still.
And some we see
in a passing glimpse
in a hurried moment
look known, familiar
like age-old friends.

## Clipped Wings

Those blue eyes
with a soft melting look
revealed a score of lovers
they had caressed or seduced

one more casualty—

he didn't think so
he could withstand temptation

her eyes melted the ice
faster than he thought—

the seductive moment
changed the course of his life

after the lapse of so many years
the blue eyes, turned somewhat grayish,
not without holding many more
had still kept him bewitched,

he didn't know
whether it was
attachment to the cage
or some sort of witchery
that had immobilized his move
or clipped his wings.

## Time Comes Tiptoeing

The breeze hovers round the flower
caresses it with a soft touch
makes it sway with joy
inhales and holds its smell—
looks like a genuine bond of love
not a wayward whimsical fling.

Time comes tiptoeing, unseen
the breeze rudely shakes the flower
makes it shiver with fright
scatters its petals around
as if love were just a whim
and the bond a tender, brittle thing.

Soft eyes meet, hearts respond
lovers quiver with immense joy
each one is the other's dream
happy to be joined in marriage—
looks like a genuine bond of love
not a wayward impulsive thing.

Time comes tiptoeing, unseen
soft looks change to a harsh glare
bodies shake with intense rage
each one becomes a nightmare
relieved to break off the marriage
as if love were just a whim
and the bond a tender, brittle thing.

# The Mirror Doesn't

The mirror just reflects
the face of a truthful man

the mirror doesn't hear
that only a minute ago
he asked his growing son
to tell the "man on the phone"
that daddy wasn't home.

The mirror just reflects
the face of a faithful lady

the mirror didn't see
that only a moment ago
she phoned her secret friend
to tell him she was alone
and the husband won't be home.

The mirror just reflects
the expression of the face
the mirror doesn't know
the secrets of the heart.

## A Smile Is A Smile

Her face had the glow of fulfillment
and the sheen of spousal pride
when she caught, imaged in the mirror,
the smile on her man's face
—a happy, settled man—
as she turned to the kitchen chores.

His was a smile of satisfaction
—a mark of great relief—
at his return to a cozy home
and a grateful, contented wife,
after an undetected tryst
with a luscious paramour.

## Adolescence

Lately whatever he did—
walking his dog, reading a book,
listening to his favourite songs—
he saw her young, girlish face
with her quiet, lovely eyes.
Or her walk, curls bouncing
onto her dimpled cheeks,
her smile,
the soft corner lift
of her upper lip.

His activities, interspersed
with stray, recurring visions
of hers,

not once did they date,
just sat side by side
in their class
at school.

Wherefrom came
all these silly thoughts,
he shrugged his shoulders
and asked
no one in particular

Is it love?

# I'll Err Again

If loving you is erring, I'll err again
let those who differ complain
but tell me if you can—

Should not the parched earth love the rain?
Should not the rain love the clouds?
Should not the clouds love the vaporous mist?
Should not the vapors love the sun?

Water is ripple in the river
    moisture in the air
    clouds in the skies
    rain on the ground.

How can water not be water
or cease to love its forms?

Let me tell you if I can
let those who differ complain
if loving you is erring, I'll err again.

## Will You Not Think Of Me?

When you lie in affectionate arms,
tasting of life and love and hope,
and look at the vast starlit skies,
with the moon shining full and bright,
will you not think of me, oh dear?
For I likened your eyes to the stars,
and your winsome face to the moon.

Standing at the window of wedding chamber,
when you watch the dim light of dawn,
with eye's still heavy with the night's sleep,
half-opened in the freshness of morn,
will you not think of me, oh dear?
For I likened the opening of your eyes
to the magic of the break of dawn.

Lying of the petals of roses red,
with the light breezes whispering by,
with his fingers on your ruby lips,
when someone talks of love to you,
will you not think of me, oh dear?
For I likened your lips to roses red,
and your breath to fragrant breezes.

While walking through an autumnal
      wood,
with arms love-locked, hand in hand,
over withered leaves which once were
      green,
when someone talks of hope of morrow,
will you not think of me, oh dear?
For in the autumnal life of mine,
you once came with the hope of spring.

# Expressions

Softer than the petals of a rose
gentler than the flakes of snow

sharper than shards of glass
keener than the edge of a sword

are words, spoken or said—

but softer, gentler

sharper, keener

are the quiet glances
of expressive eyes—

which soothe

or sting

more than the spoken word.

## Words Left Unsaid

There's so much to say—

so much is left unsaid
to be thought over
resulting in delay
and regret.

Moments are passing birds
perch on the chimney once
for a moment or so
to rest their tired wings
then hastily fly away
to return no more.

Words left unsaid
of love, lapse or regret
are like moments
that pass you by.

But unlike them
come back to haunt
the slow, sad penitent.

## Un-Relieved Pain

Wish one could pack up
the remnants of un-relieved pain
tie them up in a secure sack,
and leave them at the curb for the truck
to haul it to the outskirts
of the town
to dump and bury it
deep and down
into the inaccessible recesses
of the ground
making sure, no burning
or the acrid smoke
coiling up in the air
could waft back to the town
and make the whole effort
go up in smoke,
resurrecting the old emotional hurt
and a resurgent spurt of pain.

## A Tear Drop

Such versatility
in a tiny drop
of saline water
expressive of the widest
range of emotions—

a marvel of compression;
an ocean in a drop—

Joy and success
and despair, no less
failure, hurt and grief
or a sigh of relief
all rolled into
a small tiny blob—

a wonder of brevity;
a symphony in a note—

A wordless mode
a silent medium
with such eloquence
as no words can reach
or match.

## A Changed Focus

Soaked with sorrow are the sentiments
dripping with sadness are the words
over the lapse of what was once
the good old times of togetherness.

Never was this song a song of loss
for the melodic tune and the sound of music
were hauntingly engaging with the sweetness then,
the sentiments underneath never touching us
while we just hummed along to the rhythmic song.

The awareness now is of the pathos of theme,
the old appeal of the lilt & beat is gone,
I sit alone, nostalgic in the familiar room
so sadly focused on the loss of you.

SECTION FOUR

*Rama*

*Went*

*Away*

## Re-Incarnation

Vultures,
pecking greedily
at the carrion,
are debauches reborn.
For, in their past birth,
their lustful hunger
for carnal pecking
seems to have been
left unsatisfied.

The flesh they touched,
nibbled or gnawed,
in their past debaucheries,
was as unresponsive
as 'tis now,
to the hungry bite
of their lustful passion.

Now re-incarnated
as vultures,
they smell and eat
the stinking carrion
lest their hunger
should be left over
for the next birth.

# Some Call Him God
## A SCIENTIST PONDERS

The universe is verily a
manifestation of energy—
matter, gas, air
solid forms or fluid
differ only in measure,
levels & degrees—
forming, reforming
grouping, regrouping
transforming from one
to the other.

energy or shakti

inert or moving
dormant or active

was always there
shall always be there—

names by which it is addressed
may be one or many
depending on one's own
sight or insight
conditioned and molded often
by culture, land or clime.

## Two For One

Like a swirl of a whirlwind
his mind moved in circles
reverting to the thought
of his friend having died
of the failure of heart.

Being much younger in years
active in sports
sensible with food—
nothing could stop his early exit.

Picture in the obituary columns
could have well been his own
if it weren't for
a timely rescue
a quick, successful operation
in his own lucky case.

His had always been the life
of a hamster on a wheel—
too busy for his wife and kid,
too occupied for proper rest.

Propped up in bed, eyes closed,
his mind now lingered
on his wife's tired eyes
ravaged by sleepless nights,
his kid's languid hands
listlessly touching his toys,
the endless calls and messages
from his neglected friends.

He surveyed his stitched up chest
thought of the repaired, re-set heart
realized how fragile existence was
how unsure one's life was
and how his priorities
had all along been slipshod.

In this fresh, renewed lease on life
he couldn't miss the finer print
that life wasn't meant just for work
it was also for leisure, play & fun.

He felt painfully sorry for his friend
who had met with an early end
who did have a chance but one,
was no less thankful for the fact
that God in His boundless mercy
had granted him two for one.

## He Would Meet Us There

Here's a land of houses of worship
the whole landscape is strewn with them
and rising from them we hear sermons
on charity, sharing, caring and love.

Do those sermons rise from the
Preachers' faith
do they touch the congregation's heart
or are those sermons part of a practiced
Art
aimed at bodies whose minds are
Elsewhere?

When words are words, bereft of sense
when sounds they make have no intent
Then the One who is known as love
And truth
in His own house shown disrespect.

Let's build places of worship and prayer
such as shelters, hospitals and food banks
where service is prayer and deeds are
Words
and wherever else God is, He would
meet us there.

# The Budda & Silence

His eyes had seen
All ecstatic joys
And all the shades
Of life, sorrow & death.

He had become
Mute with wisdom.

Wisdom spoke in silence
And silence he chose
The if's and but's
The why's and how's
Then's & now's
Now's & hereafter's
Of daily parlance
Had no relevance
For his seeing eyes
With an unseeing look.

They looked & looked
And understood
The sense & essence
of life & being.

# Commotion

The flame didn't waver
but the mind did
again and again
from the meditational focus
on the Lord's form
envisioned within.

From the serene, kind
smile on the Lord's face,
eyes brimming over
with love and compassion
and the hand
raised in benediction,
the mind retracted
again and again
and strayed on
to the daily scene
on the street
of the young, innocent kids
—such tender saplings of humankind—
with famished frames
sunken, desolate eyes
grimy hands stretched for alms
before indifferent passers by.

A pendulum
going back and forth
not knowing
how to stop.

## Clay & The Potter

Man is an amazing work of art,
no less than a wonder, an awe!
Like an artist in his art,
the Creator has left a clod
a touch of His own hands,
a ray of His own light,
a spark of His own flame
& a bit of His own make.

So unique is this body of man,
so singular is the mind therein,
and there's nothing else to match
the one sublime, matchless soul!

Though the body at times can err
and the mind may oft go astray
the spirit guides and commands
and the two have to listen and obey.

While the body walks the earth
and the mind explores the skies,
the spirit moves and waves
through the vast, edgeless void
to make, shape and guard,
as the vital force of Life.

The same force is active
through the texture of man's being.
He isn't of the earth, earthly
and he isn't only a mind.
He's a rare spiritual entity
so made by the hands Divine!

## No Fixed Address

A stray thought stirred
my meditational poise
& the suppliant me
asked the Lord
to correct my guess
and to tell me about
His true address.

"You're deluded, my child,"
He said,
"by the varied forms—
a cloud, a shower,
a hailstorm,
the ocean, river,
stream and rill,
dew on a flower,
snow on a hill
can mislead the eye,
though
its water
in varied forms.

A discerning eye
finds
the truth beneath,
a deluded sight
falters
on its depth
and height.

Realize this, my child,
I'm confined
here nor there,
at one location
or address,
people do argue or guess,

I am present
**everywhere**."

## Slicing The Air

We enclose His presence
within walls
and tend to feel free
in the outside world
unlearning fast what
we were taught inside
about honesty, love and truth.

We shut our minds
thinking Him confined
unable to watch
through the thick walls—
being smug
forgetting that the walls
were built by us
not raised by Him.

We know it's futile
to divide water
with our fingers
or slice up air
with our hands—
but not strange
to devise
to fragmentize
His omnipresence—
like trying
to retain
the grains
of sifting sand
in a porous sieve.

## A Matching Game

O God!
People play God,
claim power greater than yours.
They deal in life, like you;
you ring in one,
they wring out two.

They can, with utmost ease,
blow off entire cities,
wipe out a race or two,
change the world tapestry,
raze progress from history,
and turn the journey back to zero.

They measure your strength
in the fury of typhoons.
They perceive your power
in the havoc of hurricanes.
They reckon your prowess
in the wreckage of earthquakes.

You go a mile, they go two.
You kill people, they do too,
and they claim in clear words,
they can do better than you!

# Roll Call

The priest stands waiting in the church
& wondering
where all the people have gone tonight,
& except for the statue of Jesus, no one
    else's in sight.

Some been drinking, and being good
    citizens,
wouldn't 'drink & drive,' with blood
    alcohol levels so high.
Others are at the parties, in well packed
    halls,
clad in the glimmer & shimmer of
    carefree dresses,
& there's the flavour of food & fun &
    wine,
An' the joy & cheer of Christmas is in
    the air.

Some are at work, and others are sick,
lounging in the clinics or propped up in
    their beds.
Others are house-guests lodged in the
    jails,
relaxing & feasting at the taxpayers' fare.
Some old folks are home, grandchildren
    in their care,
& are handling the rosary, half-asleep in
    prayer.

> An' the priest stands waiting in the
> church
> & wondering
> where all the people have gone
> tonight,
> & except for the statue of Jesus, no one
> else's in sight.

## Putting Reason To Rest

He was a man of God
doing all that he could
to alleviate suffering and misery

they didn't like him

not for what he preached
or did
but because
he wasn't from their stock

he fell under their blows

with a barrel aimed at him
a look of deep compassion
rose in his eyes
as if forgiving them
for their trespass

a shot rang out and broke
the silence of the jungle—

silencing an innocent life,
and putting reason to rest.

## Balance Sheet

How am I accountable
for the failings and faults
of the forefathers

I carry their genes

But genes are not
my option
or my choice

Was it that
I was responsible
who way back
set the ball rolling
which has since been gathering mass
of Karma
of fines and fruits
birth after birth—

Anything left undone
supposed to have been done
or wrongly done
was carried forward
for completion or atonement
in the next birth—

Genes so programmed,
slips had to be mended,
rectified, over births
as many times as required
till perfection was achieved—
A state—

where Karma ceases
the genes having exhausted
the in-built programming—

And finally one is
at perpetual, peaceful rest
released
from the cycle of births
after unloading
the burden of generations.

## The Flower & The Seeker

Of the fragrance
that hovers round the flower
the flower thinks
it comes from the outside
little knowing
its nestled inside
it's very own being,
and breathes through
it's every pore.

Thinking of Him
as outside of him
a seeker errs
like the flower does.

# Rama Went Away

The bells were ringing
and the chant was on
in the Rama's temple
on a lovely morn.

Rama stood outside
& watched a young cobbler boy,
under a leafless tree
by the dusty road,
working on a rich man's shoe,
while reciting the Rama's name.

The rich man haggled and hassled,
& underpaid the young cobbler boy,
and then with his rich offerings
went inside the temple gate.

Rama saw a bejeweled lady
who came in a luxury car,
bought some strings of flowers,
and threw some coins on the vender's
mat—
less than the settled price—
much lower than the cost—
and then with her rich offerings
went inside the temple walls.

She didn't turn even once
to answer a wail of protest—
a helpless widow's call—
who recited the Rama's name
and ran the flower stall,
than beg for coins and alms.

Rama blessed those simple folks,
whose hands plied an honest trade
while their minds were fixed on him.

Glancing towards the rich folks,
Rama's smile said it all:
"Let them worship a marble block,
let them adore a piece of rock,
My temple is the human heart,
My address is the human soul."

Rama didn't go inside the temple.
Rama went away.